DISCARD

W9-BNB-612

Now and then we had a hope that if we lived and were good,
God would permit us to be pirates.
—MARK TWAIN

Neptune, the Roman god of the sea

LIVES *of the* PIRATES

Swashbucklers, Scoundrels (Neighbors Beware!)

WRITTEN BY Kathleen Krull

ILLUSTRATED BY Kathryn Hewitt

HARCOURT CHILDREN'S BOOKS

HOUGHTON MIFFLIN HARCOURT

BOSTON   NEW YORK   2010

Thanks to Christine Kettner, Regina Roff, and Sara Gillingham
for their expert design work, and to Darlene Mott of the
Sam Houston Regional Library and Research Center for helping
with information about Jean Laffite.

—K.H.

Text copyright © 2010 by Kathleen Krull
Illustrations copyright © 2010 by Kathryn Hewitt

All rights reserved. For information about permission to
reproduce selections from this book, write to
Permissions, Houghton Mifflin Harcourt Publishing Company,
215 Park Avenue South, New York, New York 10003.

Harcourt Children's Books is an imprint of Houghton Mifflin Harcourt Publishing Company.

www.hmhbooks.com

The illustrations in this book were done in oil paint on Arches paper.
The text type was set in Dante MT.
The display type was set in Captain Kidd.

Library of Congress Cataloging-in-Publication Data
Krull, Kathleen.
Lives of the pirates : swashbucklers, scoundrels (neighbors beware!) /
written by Kathleen Krull ; illustrated by Kathryn Hewitt.
p. cm.
Includes bibliographical references.
ISBN 978-0-15-205908-8 (hardcover : alk. paper)
1. Pirates—Biography—Juvenile literature. I. Title.
G535.K78 2010
910.4'5—dc22
2009019296
Manufactured in China
LEO 10 9 8 7 6 5 4 3 2 1
4500212361

R0431825542

For Katherine Thomerson,
the original pirate queen of the Frugal Frigate,
who inspired us, and for Jeannette Larson,
who guided the pirates into harbor.

—K.K. AND K.H.

CONTENTS

LIVES OF THE PIRATES

INTRODUCTION

AS SOON AS ships started sailing, people popped up to rob them. Fleeing their land-locked lives, pirates sailed the seven seas for adventures in stealing. Think outlaws. Think criminals. Violent, hairy, crude, and rude. And not all of them were men.

These were rebels, but with a cause—flouting authority, living lives as free as the wind, challenging unfair rules. (Can it be coincidence that so many pirate ships have *revenge* as part of their name?) True, they were robbers, but they were often underdogs as well, fighting against society's laws, armies and navies, and whole governments. They were bullies but also team players, governed by their own democratic rules, surviving danger in exotic island locations.

No role models here. Several did play a part in world history, but mostly these were daring and dangerous criminals who made scant contributions to civilization, unlike many famous musicians, artists, and writers. And yet—aided by the flow of entertaining pirate-themed books and movies—we continue to be fascinated with pirates, usually thinking of them in a romantic, idealistic way.

But what were they like as real people? Alas, except for the dates of their executions, hard information is difficult to come by. Usually running from the law, pirates avoided publicity. Most didn't have marriage ceremonies, own houses, pay taxes, or take notes. Essentially homeless, they didn't often have next-door neighbors who might have tattled. Respectable scholars, past and present, have tended not to devote their time to pirate research.

Instead, far from the sea, writers with brawny imaginations have sat at their desks, spinning pirate stories and embellishing them for dramatic effect. That's why we have many more myths and legends than reliable facts about pirates.

One of the two greatest myths about pirates is that they were likable swash-bucklers with a colorful way of talking—that image comes from Hollywood. We do know that real pirates were not all alike. Most did swear a lot. But which one got loot by sneaking her hand under the mattresses of sleeping captains? Who made his crew drink their own urine? Which one spent his days on deck wearing pajamas? Which one patiently pulled a parasitic worm out of his leg—all two feet of it? What was the oddest thing about our hairiest pirate? Who kept her pirate ship tethered to the bedpost in her castle? Who personally led his crew in religious services twice a day? Who provoked the most mutinies against him? And which pirate sprinkled her troops with garlic water before raids?

The second myth about piracy is that it ended centuries ago. In fact, it continues to this day, mostly in areas where crushing poverty coexists with unpoliced oceans. There are hundreds of pirate attacks on ships every year, especially around the Philippines, Indonesia, parts of South America, Nigeria, and Somalia. Now the targets are often oil and gas tankers or ships carrying drugs. We see today's pirates as thieves and murderers on the high seas—and if they operate out of political or religious beliefs, as terrorists.

Yet pirates from centuries past will always capture our imagination. Here, presented chronologically, as factually as possible (but mentioning the more credible rumors), are the lives of some twenty men and women—a gallery of villains, a journey through spectacular geography, and a window into world history.

—*Kathleen Krull*

LIVES OF THE PIRATES

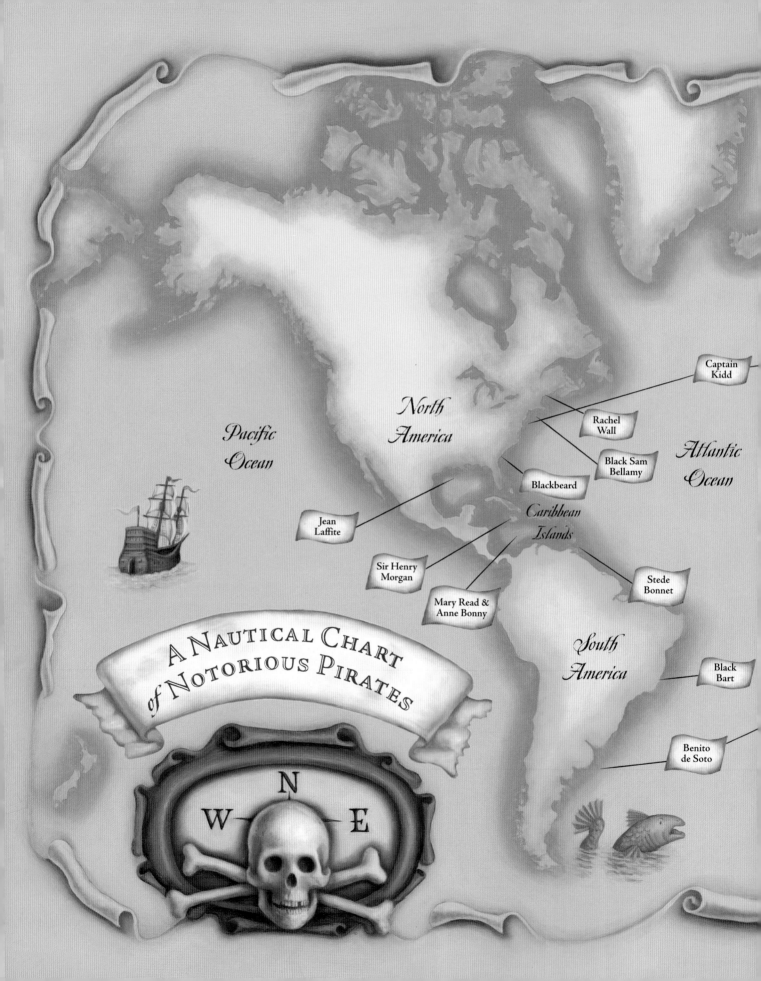

A NAUTICAL CHART
of NOTORIOUS PIRATES

Alvilda

Lady Mary
Killigrew

Grace
O'Malley

Europe

Asia

The Barbarossa
Brothers

China

Madame
Cheng

Africa

Conajee
Angria

*Indian
Ocean*

Australia

Sir Francis
Drake

William
Dampier

Alvilda

MID-400s

Scandinavian princess-turned-pirate

ALVILDA was a wild young princess of the Goths, an East Germanic tribe that lived in what is now Sweden. Her father, king of the Goths, arranged an excellent marriage for her to Prince Alf of Denmark. Apparently Alvilda was unenthusiastic. She ran away and became a pirate instead.

Leaving behind cozy royal robes of fox and squirrel, she dressed in men's clothes, with cold armor and a helmet. Forgoing fancy meals of whale or seal meat with berries or hazelnuts, washed down with wine or beer, she lived a harsh life on her ship. She recruited other noblewomen seeking adventure, and as a gang they raided vessels along the icy Atlantic coast. After capturing a ship whose captain had died, Alvilda took over the crew and commanded equal numbers of men and women.

Prince Alf, not taking the hint, decided to get his own ship and go pirate-hunting. After his ship followed a suspicious vessel into the Gulf of Finland, dangerous with ice, a bloody battle erupted. His men surged aboard. Alf ordered the captain to be brought before him. He removed the captain's helmet. Behold, it was Alvilda—just as he had hoped. He immediately proposed again, and this time she accepted. Alvilda retired from piracy, had a daughter, and ended up as queen of Denmark.

She may or may not have actually existed. Her story was recorded by a monk named Saxo Grammaticus, who wasn't fussy about fact or fiction in his *History of the Danes* in the Middle Ages. Women of Alvilda's era were tough, with much authority. If Saxo Grammaticus made the story up, he may have intended to warn women against straying from their "proper" role: staying home and being pretty.

But if Alvilda did exist, she was the first known female pirate. It would take another thousand years for the next rebellious woman to appear in the pirate records.

THE BARBAROSSA BROTHERS

ARUJ, 1473?–1518 · KHAIR, 1475?–1546

*Greek brothers who made the Barbary States
of North Africa notorious for piracy*

THE MUSLIM Ottoman Empire was mighty, but not powerful enough to control two red-haired pirates. And why would it? Like many pirates throughout history, the Barbarossa brothers were more of a help than a problem for those in power.

Aruj and Khair grew up in a haven for local pirates, the Greek island of Lesbos. They were two of four sons born to a Muslim retired soldier and a Christian Greek woman said to be the widow of a priest. As Aruj and Khair grew older and sprouted carrot-colored beards, Barbarossa ("Red Beard") became their mutual nickname.

The four brothers worked first as sailors. Some of them turned pirate to counter the raids by the Knights of St. John, who were Christian pirates operating out of the island of Rhodes. One brother was killed, another disappeared, and then Aruj was captured by the Knights, imprisoned, and sold as a galley slave.

His younger brother Khair, meanwhile, was learning six languages and becoming an outstanding engineer.

Aruj managed to escape and make his way to Egypt. The sultan, readying a fleet of ships to send to India, put one under Aruj's command. Aruj sent for Khair, found a crew of sailors, and joined the centuries-long holy war between Christians and Muslims. As pirates, they attacked ships and islands of the Mediterranean controlled by Christians.

Their most valuable prizes were people, many of whom were then enslaved in the city of Algiers, capital of Algeria in North Africa. At one time, Algiers claimed to have thirty thousand slaves, the most famous being Miguel Cervantes, who escaped and later wrote *Don Quixote*. On their ships, the Barbarossas used slaves to row their speedy galleys. Swiftness was a major weapon in their hit-and-run attacks.

Although Khair was the engineer, it was Aruj who figured out how to attach sails to cannons to help propel the weapons across the deserts of North Africa to his ships. In one battle a cannonball tore off his arm. But he grew powerful enough to take over the fabled walled city of Algiers, full of fountains, ornate mosques, and public baths. He had his opponents killed and declared himself sultan of Algiers. When he later surrendered this title to the Ottomans, they gratefully bestowed on him another grand title and promised to support him. Leaving Khair in charge of affairs in Algiers, Aruj sailed on to take over other towns.

Soon Algiers, Morocco, and Tripoli so tolerated and even encouraged piracy

that the area came to be known as the dreaded Barbary States of North Africa. Technically, North Africa belonged to the Ottoman, or Turkish, Empire. But the empire did little to stop the Barbarossas, because they were helping establish Ottoman control.

Finally, Spain sent a force specifically to target Aruj. After a six-month siege, he was killed at about age forty-five.

Khair carried on. The Ottomans appointed him commander of their navy. He won one fierce battle after another, at one point sacking the Spanish island of Majorca and taking six thousand captives. His fleet of thirty-six ships sailed home (raiding three islands along the way) to a giant victory parade in what is now Istanbul. After dictating five volumes of his memoirs—there was a lot to tell—Khair died peacefully at about age sixty-five in his palace on the Bosporus.

For the next several hundred years, Barbary pirates were unstoppable. Not until the 1800s did American, British, Dutch, and French forces combine to suppress them.

LADY MARY KILLIGREW

ACTIVE 1530–90

Part of an English husband-and-wife pirate team

MOST PIRATES were unmarried, but any woman married to a pirate was definitely left behind when he went to sea. Mary Killigrew was an exception. Her father was a pirate, she married a pirate, and her son John was a pirate. Mary did not want to be left behind.

Piracy was almost respectable among the well-to-do along the remote coast of Cornwall, England. It was just one of the Killigrew businesses, like being a musician or serving England as a diplomat or soldier. The family's castle, Pendennis, was perfectly placed at the mouth of Falmouth Harbor. For stashing loot, Lord Killigrew built a giant fortified house nearby, with a secret passage leading right to the harbor. Without anyone really caring, Lord and Lady Killigrew profited for years by selling items they retrieved from ships, sunken and otherwise. Even Queen Elizabeth I tended to tolerate pirates during peacetime, because if war came they could prove valuable.

While her husband was leading attacks at sea, Mary's job was to sort the stolen goodies and sell them around Ireland and southwest England. Neighbors reported that she oozed charm as a hostess, serving pastries and other good food and drink to her pirate crews.

One night, heavy storms drove a Spanish merchant ship into Falmouth Harbor. Lady Killigrew, now masterminding attacks, led a group—two of her servants and five Flemish sailors—onto the ship. They killed the entire crew and stole every bit of goods: rolls of precious cloth, money, even six leather chairs. Neighbors noticed she later had the chairs removed from her sight and buried in the garden, perhaps out of guilt.

The two owners of the Spanish ship were outraged and complained to authorities. But the president of the Cornwall Commission for Piracy was none other than Mary's son John. He pointed out that there were no surviving witnesses and ruled that unknown persons had carried out the attack. The Spanish owners took their case all the way to Queen Elizabeth, who grew testy when pirates stirred up trouble with neighboring countries. The case was heard in court and Mary was sentenced to death for piracy. Her two servants were hanged, yet she still had an influential friend or two—and she went free.

Pirating agreed with her. A few years later, she organized another group to raid a German ship. They killed two of its crew, retrieving barrels of silver coins. Mary was arrested, and this time her chances looked bleak. But loyal John, doing well as a pirate, paid some hefty bribes, and at her trial the jury acquitted her.

It's believed she then retired. John kept going well into the 1600s, with his wife joining him, continuing the Killigrew married-couple pirate tradition.

GRACE O'MALLEY

1530?–1603?

Irish noblewoman with one of the longest pirate careers ever

LEGENDS STILL circle Grace O'Malley. Did she really have deep scars in her forehead because she dared to attack eagles when she was a child? Did she amass and bury more than nine tons of treasure? Give birth on a ship while it was being attacked by Barbary pirates?

We know that Grace O'Malley never took no for an answer. She started her pirate career as a teen, probably dispensing with school. The story is that she begged to go on a trading trip to Spain with her father, "Black Oak" O'Malley. When he argued that her long hair would catch in the ship's ropes, she hacked it off. Her family started calling her "Grace the Bald." Undeterred, she learned to be an expert sailor.

The O'Malleys were a seafaring clan, with a motto of "Powerful by land and by sea." They ate a lot of fish: herring, salmon, cod. They always had better furniture and drank better wines than their neighbors because they did more than fish: they taxed or just plain robbed any ship that passed by. Their three-story castle on the isolated, rugged moors of Clare Island was cold and damp but provided a perch from which to pounce on ships en route to Galway. They and their crew would lurk in inlets not yet on any map, take what they wanted from a ship, and then let it pass. Other family activities included gambling with dice (a favorite game of Grace's), partying with traveling musicians, feasting on meats and vegetables and mead, and feuding with neighbors.

Some sixty independent Irish tribes, ruled by chieftains such as Black Oak

O'Malley, were in a constant state of war. At the same time, they battled the English government as it tried to impose its rule. Black Oak was one of the few chieftains who never caved in to England, and his only child, Grace, had his ferocious spirit.

Her first marriage was at sixteen, to "Donal of the Battles," one of the neighbors. While he continued his reckless tribal attacks, she raised three children. She was supposed to be making meals, keeping the castle clean, perhaps doing some charity work, but instead she started robbing ships. When Donal left her a widow in her thirties, his enemies promptly attacked their home, known as Cock's Castle. Grace repelled them so neatly that the residence became known as Hen's Castle. Later, when English forces tried to seize the castle, she ran out of ammunition while defending it. She had its metal roof torn off and melted down, then poured the scalding liquid metal from the ramparts onto English heads.

After her father died, Grace assumed command of his fleet. Fewer than one hundred people lived on Clare Island—not enough to notice her stepping up raids, with hauls of silk, salt, wine, steel. Working between three and twenty ships at a time, leading raids from Scotland to Spain, she had two hundred loyal men in her command. They were mostly other O'Malleys, plus some of Donal's men. Historians continue to marvel that any man followed a woman's leadership during this era. Perhaps Grace was simply formidable, a bully used to getting her own way. Or maybe she was inspirational, so extraordinarily successful as a pirate that it was better to be with her than anyone else.

Grace's second marriage was to a man who always wore a coat of mail and was called Iron Richard. A wealthy woman now, she was mostly interested in his castle nestled in heather-covered hills: Rockfleet Castle offered a more sheltered haven for her work. It was rumored that every night she ran a rope through a hole in her bedroom wall, attaching her favorite boat to her bedpost. According to local laws she and Iron Richard married for one year—a sort of trial marriage that gave a couple the chance to call it off. It's said that when the year was up Grace divorced Richard and kept the castle, locking him out and calling, "I dismiss you!" from the ramparts above. Nevertheless, they seem to have stuck together for years after, until his death. They had one son, known as Toby of the Ships.

Grace never called herself a pirate, referring to her job as "maintenance by land and sea." She did get caught raiding once and was arrested as a "director of thieves and murderers at sea." Three men arrested with her were executed, but after a grueling year and a half in prison, Grace was let free.

The biggest thorn in her side was Richard Bingham, a provincial governor sent from England. He loathed her as a "woman who overstepped the part of womanhood." He had her son Owen killed, confiscated many of her cattle and horses, imprisoned Toby for a year, used the British Royal Navy to make her life impossible, and even built a gallows reserved exclusively for her.

One of her own sons sided with Bingham, and she fought him too, killing four of his men. Finally, at age sixty-three, she'd had enough of the strife. She sailed to London at great personal risk to try to meet with the most powerful ruler in the world.

In response, Queen Elizabeth I sent Grace a list of eighteen questions about her family and life in Ireland. Grace's answers, probably dictated to a scribe, proved shrewd, and to everyone's surprise the queen agreed to see her. Perhaps she was dying to meet this "notorious woman in all the coasts of Ireland"—someone who liked to yell and swear as much as the volatile queen did. Perhaps she couldn't resist meeting another woman her age who had fought her way to the top. In any case, the queen of England and the queen of the pirates held a legendary meeting. Grace must have been compelling, because Elizabeth agreed to instruct Bingham to "have pity on the poor aged woman" and allow her "maintenance" to continue. The queen did note mildly that Grace "hath at times lived out of order."

Grace returned to life at sea, not minding the primitive conditions aboard ship or the weathering of her face or spending time away from her several grandchildren. She died at age seventy-three, having outlasted and outsailed all her enemies.

BURIED TREASURE

Residents at Howth Castle, north of Dublin, still set out an extra chair and place setting at meals. That's because one day Grace was traveling by, needing a rest. The lord of Howth refused to feed her or even let her inside. She promptly kidnapped his grandson and held him until the lord promised to always keep a place set at his table for travelers. Forks, uncommon in Grace's day, are presumably now included.

Grace's descendants from all over the world gather for an annual reunion of the O'Malley clan not far from Clare Island, which even today has a population of only about 160. Meanwhile, nearly every year a song or a dance or a play is written about Grace, or a new boat is named after her, or her likeness is etched into Ireland's famous Waterford crystal.

SIR FRANCIS DRAKE

1540?–1596

*English navigator and raider sponsored
by Queen Elizabeth I*

FRANCIS DRAKE was good-looking—and several inches taller than the average pirate. (Most pirates were short, due to poor nutrition.)

No one thought he would amount to much. The oldest of twelve sons, he received no formal education. His father, a farmer and sheep shearer, may have also been a robber: it was said he stole a horse and assaulted a man and had to flee to avoid jail. For a time the family lived in the hull of an abandoned ship.

Luckily, when Drake was twelve his father apprenticed him to an elderly ship captain. On the tricky waters of the North Sea, Drake navigated and piloted in every kind of weather. His skills became truly remarkable. Eight years later, he was master of his own ship.

Drake became a raider in the New World, joining up with his cousin and mentor, Sir John Hawkins. In the early English slave-trading expeditions, they stole from African villages and Portuguese ships. Drake was high-energy, taking advantage of every opportunity, and cool under stress.

In an ugly battle at a Spanish port off the coast of Mexico, six English ships fought, but only his and Hawkins's escaped. Drake developed an unrelenting hatred for Spain, which was then much more powerful than England and way ahead in the race to settle the New World. His hatred had a religious element—he was a devout Protestant and detested the Catholic Spanish.

Drake went on to raid dozens of Spanish ships. In one attack he stole four chests of china dishes especially for his wife, but mostly he enriched England. Technically his pirating was illegal, because Spain and England had not declared war. But a grateful Queen Elizabeth looked the other way and commissioned him for a supersecret job: He was to find a passage through or around the New World, looking for spots to establish British colonies. She sent him off with a green silk scarf embroidered with good wishes, one of her own swords, and the understanding that he'd be pirating as he traveled.

Unlike most pirates, who had to sail whatever ships they could steal, Captain Drake had a flagship, the *Golden Hind,* specially built for fighting, plundering, and getting away fast. He started out with 170 men and boys—educated nobles, a pharmacist, a tailor, seamen who slept below deck—and a small orchestra of violins and trumpets. Although most believed they had been recruited for an exploring expedition, everyone caught on to the trip's true purpose as Drake raided every single foreign ship they passed, obtaining treasure, tools, and various necessities. All men were promised an equal share of the spoils, an offer that promoted unity and steeled them for many dangers as they proceeded to sail around the world.

Drake's other technique of ensuring loyalty was discipline. Early on, he beheaded one of the nobles on board for a variety of offenses, mainly disrespect. He held up the head and shouted, "Lo! This is the end of traitors!"

Stern as he was, his crew found him fair. "All said that they adored him," wrote one Spanish nobleman, in awe. Drake tried to be gentlemanly even with his enemies, though he didn't hesitate to use violence to get what he wanted. With native people he encountered, his goal was trading and befriending, not fighting.

He kept his crew well fed, making sure they had oranges, lemons, and other fruit when possible, which prevented scurvy, the leading pirate killer. In good times they gorged on alligator, monkey, ostrich—and even penguin. In bad times they were reduced to eating biscuits filled with worms.

Drake's habits were more refined than those of most pirates. As the captain, he dined off gold-rimmed silver plates inscribed with his name. He had his own man-servant, Diego. Everyone got together twice a day for religious services, with Drake leading them in prayer.

Late into every night, he worked in his elegantly furnished quarters on a detailed journal, recording all he did and saw. His fifteen-year-old cousin, who excelled at art, helped with the drawings. Drake always regretted not having children of his own and treated this cousin as a son.

His greatest triumph was the capture of the *Cacafuego,* a floating (if heavily armed) treasure chest, the most lucrative Spanish prize ever. Drake told the captain that he was there to "rob by command of the Queen of England." He tortured the captain's clerk to force him to reveal the hiding places of thirteen hundred bars of silver, thirteen chests of silver coins, and eighty pounds of gold. It took six days to get the loot transferred over to the *Golden Hind*.

After almost three tough years at sea, Drake sailed home with only fifty-six of his men and what has been estimated in today's money as ninety million dollars. He gave extravagant presents to the queen and all her favorites. A few refused the gifts because, as one put it, "he had stolen all he had." He bought a lavish estate, a former monastery surrounded by parkland full of deer. After fourteen years of marriage, his first wife died, and two years later he married a beautiful, wealthy woman.

For being the first Englishman to circumnavigate the world, ambitiously exploring it and producing the most accurate maps so far, the queen knighted Drake in front of cheering crowds. England loved him—except for some people who grumbled that he was an upstart commoner and a petty pirate. One noble called him "the master thief of the unknown world."

Undeterred, Drake again made history as vice admiral of the English fleet that defeated the mighty Spanish Armada. His adventures at sea, less lucky as time went on, continued until he was in his midfifties. He was always aware that he could die at any time. He was once hit by a musketball in the leg and fainted from loss of blood. In an Indian attack, he was hit twice in the head with arrows, which had to be extracted. His youngest brother, who sailed with him, caught yellow fever and died in his arms.

Drake himself died at sea of dysentery, a fever, at about age fifty-six.

Upon hearing the news of Drake's death, the bedridden king of Spain said, "It is good news, and now I will get well!"

BURIED TREASURE

For centuries after his death, his nickname *El Draco* ("the Dragon") was used as a bogeyman to terrify children in Spain. Like many pirates, Drake was hailed as a hero in his home country, while others considered him a bloodthirsty criminal.

Much to his dismay, Queen Elizabeth suppressed Drake's journal. She even banned anyone else from writing about it, for fear the information would help Spain. Not until thirty-two years after his death was it published, incompletely, as a way of rousing English patriotism during a later war against Spain. Drake's original charts and journals disappeared. But he had also given out information disguised in code, which has been deciphered only in recent years.

Sir Henry Morgan

1635?–1688

Welsh pirate who went from "terror of the Spanish Main"
to governor of Jamaica

HENRY MORGAN never spoke of his childhood, which began in Wales. Was he kidnapped from his parents? Or did they actually sell him as a servant to someone in the West Indies, so he had to later purchase his own freedom? How did he end up in the humid islands?

We first meet him in Barbados at age twenty, an ordinary soldier with a great tan. He was probably part of a British force that seized Jamaica from Spain and made it an English colony. Great Britain was attempting to take over all of the Spanish Main, the Spanish colonies in the Americas.

Barbados, lawless and wild, was called "the dunghill whereon England doth cast forth its rubbish." Almost everyone there was a criminal of some sort. Pirates contributed to the economy by raiding Spanish ships heading back to Spain with silver, gold, jewels, spices, cocoa, and other exotic island goods. There was a tavern for every thirty people. Apparently Morgan looked around at men squandering their lives and then saved up his money and bought a ship of his own. Presto! He was a pirate. Actually, Morgan couldn't abide being called a pirate and considered himself a patriot.

With a reputation as a clever leader, persuasive in English and fluent in French, Morgan rose to the top of the "dunghill." From the pirate base at Port Royal, he started attacking Spanish towns in Central America on orders from Jamaica's governor. That was his good pal Sir Thomas Modyford, who'd brought one thousand English settlers with him and was anxious to get cocoa and sugar cane planted on land taken from Spain.

According to his orders, when Morgan attacked a ship at sea he had to split his booty with the English government, so he tried to attack on land when possible. He grew fabulously wealthy, bought one plantation after another, and paid for the construction of the local church. He started dressing better, in linen pants, silk coats, a vest trimmed with silver. In formal situations he covered his short hair with a wig; on ships he donned a red scarf. He was never seen without his sword. He married his cousin Mary. To his regret, they had no children.

At his peak he commanded two thousand uncouth pirates on thirty-eight ships. The only woman on board any of them was an elderly Englishwoman reported to be a witch, who gave them advice. Just keeping everyone fed was a headache, as was keeping the peace. Once, when angry men accused him of cheating them, Morgan had himself strip-searched, then humiliated them by insisting that they do the same.

With sheer boldness, sneaking his men in on canoes, he stormed the well-fortified city of Portobello. He used the city's priests and nuns as human shields to protect his men. He went on to raid wealthy Spanish settlements on the coast of Venezuela. Finally, Morgan set out to capture Panama, the city richest in gold and silver. He had to take troops through dangerous swampland, where they fought off scorpions, mosquitoes, alligators, and snakes, as well as such jungle ailments as foot rot. Though weakened, his men took over Panama, which burned to the ground while they looted it. For days they tortured the wealthy residents, in search of their hidden treasure.

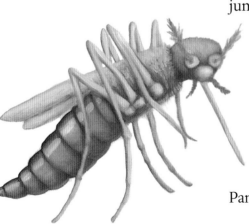

After his celebratory return to Jamaica, Modyford tsk-tsked at Morgan, but didn't punish him, merely suggesting that Morgan stop using torture.

Unfortunately for the two pals, the sack of Panama violated a peace treaty between England and Spain.

Morgan and Modyford were arrested and shipped back to England. With the help of friends who considered him a brilliant commander, Morgan was able to prove he'd had no knowledge of the treaty. King Charles II certainly didn't mind being enriched by Morgan. Plus, by never losing a battle, Morgan was helping to establish the English presence in the Caribbean. So instead of being punished, he was knighted, given a snuffbox with the face of the king set in diamonds, and shipped back to Jamaica as its governor.

But Morgan also had enemies in high places who liked to tattle about his gambling and drinking. "In his drink," wrote one, "Sir Henry reflects on the government, swears, damns and curses most extravagantly." After a year of complete control of Jamaica, he was demoted and replaced by a rival.

Drinking often got him into trouble. Once, during a serious party, he narrowly escaped death when his latest flagship, the *Oxford*, blew up accidentally. The explosion threw him into the sea and killed most of the 350 onboard.

Songs and poems detailed Morgan's exploits. A Dutch sailor, one of many who accused him of cheating his crews, wrote a bestseller called *History of the Buccaneers of America*. Greatly exaggerating his cruelty, the book made Morgan probably the most famous pirate ever known at the time. He immediately sued the book's publisher for libel, asking for a retraction and a huge sum. Morgan wasn't worried about the atrocities he was accused of; it was the book's hint of a humble background that sent him over the edge. The jury awarded him only a fraction of what he wanted, but it was the first successful libel suit in history. Later editions of the book had to include that "he was gentleman's son of good quality . . .

and was never a servant unto anybody in his life."

After some ten years as a pirate, Morgan stopped at age

thirty-nine—one of the few pirates in history who was able to retire and enjoy his wealth. He was comfortable mingling with nobles, but he also spent entire days in lowlife bars such as the Cheshire Cheese, the Cat and Fiddle, or the Green Dragon. There he would drink rum and rant.

He died in his fifties and received a twenty-two-gun salute and a state funeral. Among the possessions he left behind were 30 guns, 39 pairs of shoes, 109 slaves, 123 books, and 640 gallons of rum.

BURIED TREASURE

In 1944, a company began to market Captain Morgan rum in honor of Morgan's favorite beverage. Distilled from sugar cane and flavored with Caribbean spices, it is now one of the best-selling alcoholic drinks in the world.

In 2004, an international expedition located the wreck of Morgan's doomed ship, the *Oxford*. The government of Haiti gave permission to one company to explore it, but has since complained that American and European divers are looting the underwater wreck illegally.

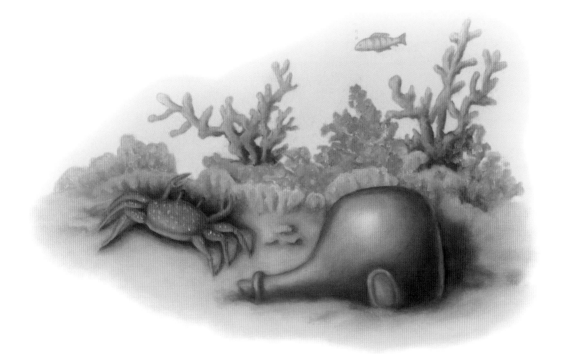

I Swear I Am Not a Pirate

Captain Kidd

1645?–1701

Doomed Scottish-American sea captain in the wrong places at the wrong times

CAPTAIN KIDD is infamous for swashbuckling his way around the world, burying tons of ill-gotten treasure along the American coast, and being venomous beyond belief.

Yet William Kidd may merely have been hard to like. His first appearance in pirate history was when he was in his midforties, upon the occasion of his entire crew deserting him. He had helped steal a ship, shrewdly renaming it *Blessed William* after the new king William III, and become its captain. In the war between England and France, he scored points for patriotism by rescuing some English ships stolen by the French. But not long afterward, his crew took off with his ship and loot, stranding him in the Caribbean.

Kidd's beginnings in Scotland were respectable—his father was a Presbyterian minister who died when Kidd was five. As a young man he headed out to sea and floated about in the free-form world of pirates for the next thirty years.

After grateful English officials replaced *Blessed William* with another ship, he tried to get respectable again, emigrating to New York City. He married the wealthiest widow in New York, twenty-year-old Sarah, eleven days after the death of her husband.

Presenting himself as a prosperous New York merchant as well as an honest, hard-working ship captain, Kidd befriended the most prominent citizens he could. Several governors called him "trusty and well beloved." He had nice houses on Pearl

Street and Wall Street, with fine furnishings, a rare Turkish carpet, silver spoons and knives (but only one fork). Out to impress, he bought a family pew at Trinity Church. He and his wife were eventually joined by two daughters, Elizabeth and Sarah.

The sea still lured him, and a fabulous opportunity knocked. Highly placed officials in America and England (including King William himself) commissioned Kidd to sail to the Indian Ocean and capture some of those dreadful pirates, as well as their loot.

His new ship, the *Adventure Galley,* was well equipped for the task, with 34 cannons, oars designed for quick getaways, and 152 treasure-hunters he personally selected. He promised crew members sixty percent of the loot—though he'd already promised sixty percent to his supporters at home, so he was either bad at math or planning to double-cross people. The crew included at least two father-and-son pairs, and at least three boys between the ages of twelve and fourteen. Everyone received a box of weapons from Kidd.

Conditions onboard quickly turned grim. Water went slimy; lice and cockroaches were in control. Kidd soon lost a fifth of his crew to scurvy and cholera. The brand-new ship sprang one leak, and then more. Keeping it afloat required the labor of eight angry men pumping water out all day and all night.

Most irritating to the crew was Kidd's caution. He failed to attack several ships, even when good prospects sailed by. The *Adventure Galley* was having no adventures.

Kidd seemed confused about his mission to capture real pirates. The one time he encountered one, he went drinking with him instead.

Some of the crew deserted when the ship was anchored offshore. Others talked of mutiny; anyone Kidd caught mentioning it was whipped. As the pressure mounted, the large and aggressive Kidd got into brawls with his own men. One sailor reported that Kidd used any excuse to "knock out their brains." Escapees told of being hoisted up by the arms and hit with swords when they were caught.

One tense day, Kidd argued with his gunner, William Moore, one of the mutiny-minded crew. After some strong words, Kidd upended a wood and iron bucket on Moore's head. The blow fractured Moore's skull, and he died the next day. Always bragging loudly about his friends in high places, Kidd invoked them again, swearing he wouldn't get punished.

He wasn't doing much raiding, but rumors spread that he was. His exploits grew more vicious with each telling. When ships could avoid crossing paths with his, they did.

Knowing that his situation was getting ticklish, Kidd became desperate. He finally seized several small ships, and then hit the jackpot: the *Quedagh Merchant*, an Armenian ship loaded with valuable silks, satins, gold, silver, opium—a wonderful array of East Indian merchandise.

By the time Kidd sailed home, still believing that he had been following

his orders, only 20 of his original 152 men were still loyal to him. Even worse, official attitudes had changed during the almost three years he was at sea. On his way into New York City, he learned that he was the target of an all-out manhunt by the governments of America, England, and India. When news of his jackpot reached England, along with those tales of torture, Kidd was declared a pirate, and the worst one of all.

After being met by his daughters and his wife (probably transferring some of his loot to her), he was promptly arrested. Under heavy guard, he was shipped to London to be tried for piracy on the high seas—and for the murder of William Moore.

He spent a year in solitary confinement in miserable Newgate Prison before his trial, writing frantic letters claiming his innocence. Rumors ran rampant in taverns and other places people gathered to gossip, crediting him with the demented deeds of others.

No one was on Kidd's side. His backers turned against him, out of embarrassment and the fear that if he were left alive he'd incriminate them.

At his trial, of which the outcome was never in doubt, two sets of papers that might have helped his case were conveniently missing. He also made a predictably poor impression. One English official said, "I thought him only a knave. I now know him to be a fool as well."

At age fifty-six, Kidd was hanged. His body was covered in tar for preservation, wrapped in chains to keep its shape, then suspended in an iron cage over the river Thames. It remained there for years, a visible warning to anyone passing by in a boat.

Until his dying day, Captain Kidd denied that he was a pirate. His excuse was always that anything illegal he'd done had been forced on him by his crew. His last words at his trial were "I am the innocentest person of them all."

Sarah, meanwhile, quietly set about retrieving as much of her husband's treasure as she could. The English government turned part of its share over to Greenwich Hospital for elderly navy men, and the rest seemed to evaporate.

BURIED TREASURE

Accused of every crime in pirate history, Kidd achieved huge fame in story and song. The very day of his execution, a ballad was published: "Captain Kidd's Farewell" is a bitter, rambling speech full of swearing. Another ballad, "The Dying Words," supposedly expressing his repentance, was printed in hymnals up until the 1900s. Not until the 1920s were biographies published that showed him as more of a scapegoat than anything.

In 1910, more than two hundred years after they were needed, the papers missing from Kidd's trial turned up, misfiled with other random government papers in a London building.

Captain Kidd may have been the only pirate who ever buried his treasure. The legend that he buried gold and silver on Long Island is the origin of the myth that many pirates bury their loot. To this day, there are constant treasure hunts in any place he visited. In 1983, two men were arrested while looking for his treasure in the South China Sea—one place he never went.

THE PIRATE WHO KEPT A DIARY
WILLIAM DAMPIER

1651–1715

Well-educated Englishman who made contributions to science when not raiding ships

WILLIAM DAMPIER'S attitude toward travel was unusual (for a pirate): "I was well satisfied enough knowing that, the further we went, the more knowledge and experience I should get."

His love of new sensations distracted him from his quest to score valuable Spanish treasure. There was so much to marvel at: the taste of a fresh yellow frog in Vietnam, the spiky iguanas and birds with red throat pouches of the Galápagos, the tang of mango pickle in the Philippines, the shocking bound feet of girls in China.

Dampier's father, a wealthy farmer in Somerset, England, had educated him at local schools; the son mastered the unpiratical subjects of Latin and math. After he was orphaned at age sixteen, he went to sea. He served in the Royal Navy in the Third Anglo-Dutch War and turned up in Jamaica at age twenty-two.

Dampier had been trying to make his fortune in the brutal trade of cutting logwood, a valuable timber. Then he lost all of his equipment in a storm. He had months of work with nothing to show for it but impressive muscles—and a diary about long walks he'd been taking around the Gulf of Mexico. In it he described hairy sloths, manatees, gangs of up to thirty angry spider monkeys, armadillos with hard shells but "very sweet" meat, velvety spiders "as big as a man's fist." He made careful observations of native peoples, currents and other phenomena at sea, and weather, including the first accurate description of a hurricane. He wrote about stumbling over fierce alligators, tasting yellow snakes, smelling whole bushes of perfumy vanilla, and discovering the best way to drink cocoa.

After the logwood failure, turning pirate wasn't a hard decision for Dampier. He teamed up with a ragtag group of some eighty men and began raiding villages and ships all over the world. In his diary he took pains to distance himself from "these pirating fellows." But he was as greedy and violent as the others, or they would have cast him out. During one storm when he was sure he was going to die, he had repentant thoughts about this "roving course of life," looking back "with horror and detestation on actions" he'd taken. But that mood soon passed.

Piracy was a way to keep his independence and to keep observing. Writing down all he saw became his obsession.

Despite the cramped conditions of a ship, every night he would find a spot to write, usually out on the open deck. He would retrieve the box where he kept a quill pen and parchment paper, sharpen the pen with a knife, make a batch of ink, write, and then get everything back into the box. No matter what peril he was in, he never left his papers behind. Keeping them safe and dry was a constant worry. In storms or during misadventures down rivers, he rolled them up and stored them inside a hollow bamboo tube with wax plugging both ends.

In one close call, his boat capsized before he had a chance to get to his papers.

He spent the next three days frantically making fires to dry them out, page by page, leaving boat repair to the less literary pirates.

Back in England after nine years as a pirate, still clutching his journals, Dampier was penniless. He married Judith, who may have been lady in waiting to a duchess. Then he promptly left the country again and spent the next twelve years at sea.

His curiosity drove him to become the first person to voyage around the world three times. The circumstances ranged from illegal to legal— sometimes he was a pirate, and once was captain of his own ship in the Royal Navy. Though brilliant at navigating, he was not a good leader. He tended to pout, saying things like "I told you so" or "If you know so much, you take charge of the ship." Some officers detested him, including his second in command, who said he "did not care a fart" for Dampier. Losing his temper one day, Dampier beat this man with his cane, put him in chains, and left him screaming "Old pirating dog!" in a Brazilian jail.

Upon his return to England, Dampier was court-martialed for cruelty, found guilty, docked three years' pay, and dismissed from the Royal Navy, declared unfit to command.

He did succeed in publishing his thrill-a-minute diaries. *A New Voyage Round the World* was an immediate bestseller. It inspired some men to take up sea life and others to pursue research in the various new branches of science. His journeys inspired two more books—he was the first Englishman to explore Australia and map it, naming places for himself along the way. He never made much money from his writing. Ironically, others stole his work and published "pirated" editions of their own.

He remained tolerant and open-minded toward other cultures, and without superstition (unlike most people of his day). He would eat or drink or experience anything. He told about tasting locusts, a plate of flamingo tongues, breadfruit, smelly durian fruit, and soy sauce. Resourceful and calm, he had unusual stamina. He did bloodletting on himself for medical reasons, was buried up to the neck in hot sand for half an hour to purge a fever, and once unspooled a two-foot-long guinea worm from his leg.

We know little about his quiet last years in London except that he never did get rich. Two years after he died at about sixty-three, his share of the money from his last voyage finally arrived. It went to pay off debts.

BURIED TREASURE

Later British writers met with financial success by borrowing freely from Dampier's journals. Twenty years after its publication, Dampier's first volume inspired Daniel Defoe's classic *Robinson Crusoe*. The title character was based on Alexander Selkirk, a Scottish sailor marooned after a disagreement with one of Dampier's men, and years later rescued by Dampier.

A hundred years after Dampier's death, an explorer wrote, "It is not easy to name another voyager or traveler who has given more useful information to the world." In the *Oxford English Dictionary*, he gets credit for introducing more than one thousand words to the language. He provided a wealth of data about the natural world that later scientists could study. In particular, he influenced the biologist Charles Darwin and his *Origin of the Species* (1859). In his own diary, Darwin affectionately called him "old Dampier."

In 1907 a plaque was installed at Dampier's church in his hometown. Some locals protested bitterly, one calling him "a pirate ruffian that ought to have been hung."

JUST PLAIN TERRIFYING

BLACKBEARD

(EDWARD TEACH)

1680?–1718

*English pirate so intimidating that
victims surrendered at the sight of him*

TWO THINGS stand out about Edward Teach: how he looked and how he died.

He was tall, broad shouldered, notably strong, dressed in rough clothes and a fur cap. It was his intensely black beard, long and bushy, that made everyone call him Blackbeard. One early writer dubbed his beard a "frightful meteor" that covered his whole face. He liked to call attention to it by sectioning it into odd little tails tied up with ribbons. For a truly diabolical effect, he lit matches and twisted them into his hair when he invaded a ship. He would also sprinkle gunpowder on his rum, set it on fire, and drink it down as he came aboard. Making people twitch helped him do his job, and Blackbeard's image screamed "pirate."

Born in Bristol, England, he started his career serving on Jamaican ships raiding the French and Spanish. Benjamin Hornigold, a prominent pirate of the day, taught him everything he knew, and in his late thirties Blackbeard struck out on his own. He captured a boat for himself, a French slave ship he renamed *Queen Anne's Revenge*. Installing forty cannons and gathering three hundred pirates on several more ships, he cruised around, scaring people and seizing sugar, cocoa, gold dust, coins, and jewels. An excellent navigator, he had not one but two headquarters, the Bahamas in winter and the Carolinas in summer, for year-round pirating.

His usual technique was to take everything of value off a ship and, if there was no resistance, let the ship and its crew go. On ships that resisted, all aboard were killed, though there is no evidence that he personally killed anyone.

In his most confident move, Blackbeard parked his ships in the harbor of Charleston, South Carolina, virtually blockading the city. He seized eight ships and then kidnapped some eighty important citizens. He could have demanded anything he wanted as ransom, but his most pressing need was for a chest of medical supplies, reportedly including mercury for syphilis. As five days ticked by, his hostages became frantic, but when he got the supplies he released them unharmed. This episode sealed his reputation as a serious threat to the new colonies, capable of taking over even a major settlement such as New York or Boston.

With his crew, Blackbeard was magnetic and disciplined on some days, nasty on others. According to legend, he shot his own first mate in the knee, saying that if he didn't shoot one or two crew men now and then, they'd forget who he was. Another time he dared his men to accompany him below deck. He closed the hatches, filled several pots with sulfur and other flammable substances, and set the contents of the pots on fire. As the hold filled with fumes, the men coughed and gasped, hurrying back on deck for fresh air. Blackbeard was the last to emerge, snarling about what cowards they were.

At one point, feeling a need to downsize, he deliberately ran *Queen Anne's Revenge* into a sandbar. He quickly got his booty onto another ship and took off, marooning a large part of his furious crew.

Blackbeard sold some of his ships and bought a house in Bath Towne, then one of the few towns in North Carolina. He plied the governor with gifts in exchange for an official pardon and unofficial protection. He merged into fine society, entertaining lavishly, mingling with landowners and officials. We know he could read and write, but whether he really kept a journal in which he wrote things like "such a day—rum all out" is open to question. It was rumored that he got married, to Mary, the sixteen-year-old daughter of a plantation owner. Perhaps he even took a razor to his beard.

Yet something about Blackbeard's retirement from piracy seemed fake. His hilltop house, one of only two dozen houses in the area, allowed him to observe ships passing through nearby Ocracoke Inlet. It would be the perfect spot to forcibly collect a few tolls, support his lifestyle, maybe make a comeback.

Some upright citizens of North Carolina grew panicky, fearing Blackbeard's reported power to attract thousands of men into a new pirate haven. They appealed to the governor of Virginia to rid them of "this nest of vipers."

Soon Robert Maynard, a lieutenant of the British Royal Navy, was on his way to Ocracoke with a disciplined crew of sixty, prepared to eliminate Blackbeard no matter what. He found Blackbeard anchored at sea with a crew of nineteen, bleary from partying all night.

At first Blackbeard's knowledge of the inlet helped him escape, but not for long. While giving chase, Maynard ordered most of his own crew below deck.

Cornering the pirate, he tricked him into thinking the nearly empty ship was safe to board. There was a shouted exchange between captains during which Blackbeard yelled, "Cowardly puppies!" When he and his team swarmed aboard Maynard's boat, they were instantly ambushed by the larger Royal Navy crew.

Having lived large, Blackbeard died even more notoriously. In the gory fight that followed, Maynard's men reportedly shot him five times and stabbed him more than twenty times. The deck grew slimy with blood, but still Blackbeard refused to die. Over on his own ship, one of his crew, Black Caesar, tried to set off an explosion that would have killed everyone on all of the ships and sent them out in a blaze of glory. But he was prevented by two men Blackbeard had been drinking with the night before.

One of the navy men finally wounded Blackbeard in the neck and severed the pirate's head. Many tales about this death have sprouted, including the legend that the headless body, after being thrown overboard, swam three times around the ship and then sank. Maynard installed the head on the bow of his ship. Then he divided all the gold dust, silver, and other booty among his own crew, which was strictly illegal and ended his career.

The remarkable thing about Blackbeard's dramatic story is that he was comparatively unsuccessful—for a pirate. He captured fewer than thirty ships in a short career of fifteen months. He never acquired much treasure, and despite treasure-hunters' constant digging along the banks where he sailed, nothing has ever turned up to support the claims that he buried his loot.

Still, thanks to his beard, he has an enduring reputation as a supervillain who threatened the very founding of America.

BURIED TREASURE

In 1996 a ship believed to be *Queen Anne's Revenge* was discovered near Beaufort, North Carolina. Though the evidence is not conclusive, thousands of artifacts from it are now on display at the North Carolina Maritime Museum, a major tourist attraction. Over in Hampton, Virginia, there is a Blackbeard Festival every year.

Valuing entertainment over accuracy, many of the countless Hollywood movies about pirates portray Blackbeard. Most influential is 1952's *Blackbeard, the Pirate,* in which the actor Robert Newton speaks in a way most people still think pirates talked. Blackbeard shows up in books (such as one of the Time Warp Trio books by Jon Scieszka) and on TV (episodes of *SpongeBob SquarePants* and *The Simpsons*). In 2003, many were fooled by a legend that Blackbeard used the nursery rhyme "Sing a Song of Sixpence" as a recruiting tool. This rumor had been made up by a website as a way of urging people to use common sense when evaluating the truth of urban legends.

A Red Feather in His Hat
BLACK BART
(Bartholomew Roberts)
1682–1722

Welsh pirate, deadly but also the best dressed
and most straight-laced

IT WAS PROBABLY the dizziest pirate run in history: at times Bartholomew Roberts was seizing more than one ship a day. During his four-year career, this flashy dresser captured an amazing 470 vessels, stealing the equivalent of many millions of dollars.

Roberts hadn't always dressed in red brocade jackets and ruffly white shirts. He was born into poverty and went to sea at thirteen. Later, he was the third mate aboard a slave ship when it was captured by pirates near present-day Ghana. Although he repeatedly refused his captors, he was forced to join them.

The pirate captain was killed in an island skirmish and Roberts was unanimously elected his replacement. He was a rookie, but he was also tall (for a pirate), black-haired and handsome (for a pirate), intimidating, and well-spoken—plus he could navigate with the crude instruments of the day better than anyone else. The more experienced men aboard, who called themselves the House of Lords and greeted one another with "My noble lord," liked Roberts.

He promptly led them in aggressively avenging the death of the former captain. In the dark of night, they snuck onto the island, killed much of its population, and stole anything they could carry.

Then Roberts showed off his seamanship, taking a mere three weeks to sail from Africa to Brazil and landing exactly where he predicted. Having recovered from his initial reluctance, he plunged into pirating, often with a practical purpose. One of his first hauls was a cargo of English pots and pans, and another was a ship containing ironware, household goods, and forty-five barrels of gunpowder. He took aboard only men with experience that could contribute to his crew, and no one against his will. He was always on the lookout for carpenters and coopers to make barrels, and he was desperate for surgeons, as the only other treatment for the wounded was to keep them anesthetized with rum until they died.

With nerves of steel and a knack for surprise, Roberts attacked ships that had him outgunned and outmanned. "I'll blow your brains out!" was his usual yell as he boarded a ship. His flags were particularly menacing: skulls, crossbones, hourglasses,

bleeding hearts, and other symbols of impending doom. Displaying their calm confidence, his crew took their time plundering, with nonstop "cursing and swearing, more like fiends than men," said one writer.

He was especially vengeful toward ships from countries that had tried to capture him first, such as Martinique. When he got hold of a warship carrying its governor, he hanged the unfortunate man from his own ship, then killed or tortured the crew. His preferred methods of torture were whipping, cutting off ears, and hanging men up and using them for target practice.

His biggest coup was capturing the *Sagrada Familia,* a Portuguese vessel carrying a fortune in coins, diamonds, sugar, and other goods from Brazil. After this victory he started calling himself Black Bart and polishing his image.

In an era when most pirates had one outfit and wore it until it fell apart, Black Bart was famous for his fancy clothes. During attacks he wore a lacy shirt, a formal red coat and pants, a freshly powdered wig topped by a red hat with a red feather, and a heavy gold chain with a gold cross encrusted with emeralds—it had been on its way to the king of Portugal before Black Bart seized it. A red silk shoulder sling held two expensive pistols. Carrying himself like a king, he habitually renamed each new ship *Royal Fortune.*

The only known teetotaler pirate, Roberts never indulged in alcohol, but he didn't mind when others did. Instead, he constantly drank tea from a silver tea set. He could read and write and had beautiful handwriting. He once fired off an elegant lecture to a governor: "This comes expressly from me to let you know that had you come off as you ought to have done, and drank a glass of wine with me and my company, I should not have harmed the least vessel in your harbor . . ."

Now, how could Black Bart get his large, unruly crew to work as a team? A music lover, he hired onboard musicians from which any man could request a tune, day or night. He owned several prayer books and held a worship service every Sunday. But his most famous technique was a list of eleven "shipboard articles," a code of conduct he found necessary in what he called their "abominable" profession. Each pirate had to agree to rules such as "If any man rob another he shall have his nose and ears slit." Loot was to be precisely divided among the men, depending on rank and who had suffered any injury or loss of limb. No gambling, no fighting aboard ship, lights out at eight every night. He didn't forbid his crew to drink, but if they did so after eight o'clock they had to "sit upon the open deck without lights."

Black Bart was so cool and confident that his crew never questioned his leadership, a rare feat for pirates. He kept them supplied with their favorite concoctions—black strap (a mix of rum, molasses, and beer) and rumfustion (eggs, beer, sherry, and gin heated with cinnamon, nutmeg, and brown sugar). He made sure they were fed salmagundi (all the ingredients the cook had on hand, cooked in spiced wine) and, on good days, turtle stews. During the toughest times he rationed them to one mouthful of bread a day and one swallow of water. When water ran out, they drank their own urine.

As the crew grew giddy and cocky with success, Black Bart grew crabby and irrational from the strain of controlling them. At violations of rules and at any stupidity (like the time the crew attacked wearing silly necklaces of sausages to show their contempt for their prey), he lost his temper, revealing a repertoire of curses. He shot one of his own men for drunkenly dropping a cask of water, then stabbed another man for helping the first.

His motto was reported to be "A merry life and a short one." He died abruptly at forty, during a battle with the *Swallow,* a British man-of-war that had been chasing him for eight months. In the midst of a driving storm, Black Bart had boldly ordered his ship, with its huge haul of gold dust, to sail right past the *Swallow*—but before the wind carried him away, cannonfire struck him in the throat. His mate tried to rouse him, saw he was dead, and burst into tears. The crew immediately threw his body overboard, according to his fervent wish.

Three hours later, the survivors surrendered. In a huge circus of a trial, 52 of his crew of 254 were sentenced to be hanged till they were "dead, dead, dead."

BURIED TREASURE

As for the haul of gold dust aboard Black Bart's last ship, the captain of the *Swallow* took three years to turn some of it over to the government. He kept the rest, despite repeated orders, claiming as he was knighted and eventually made commander of the Royal Navy that he needed the money to keep up his lifestyle.

It has been speculated that Black Bart was actually a woman in disguise. Besides his mysterious fastidiousness about typical pirate activities, he was always clean-shaven, with no trace of beard. He insisted on privacy in his quarters and commanded that he be immediately thrown overboard when he died.

MARY READ AND ANNE BONNY

MARY, 1685?–1721 · ANNE, 1697?–1782?

Two women, one English, one Irish, who sailed to the New World and into the pirate hall of fame

PIRATE LIFE was so strenuous that pirates often experienced hernias, all sorts of other crippling disorders, and early death. The need for brute strength was one of the reasons women didn't often join up. But nothing fazed Mary Read and Anne Bonny.

Mary Read was raised as a boy in rough-and-tumble London. Her father, a sea captain, was at sea when she was born, and her mother told him Mary was a he—a son called Mark. She wanted to ensure that they would inherit the captain's fortune. The lie worked, and the two were able to live on the inheritance after Mary's father died. Then the money ran out. Still dressed as a boy, Read found work as a servant to a French woman, but became bored and decided to go to sea. Her job was to haul gunpowder to the sailors who operated the cannons. Bored again, she joined the Flemish army, learned to use a sword, and proved herself in battle. But she gave up her disguise when she fell in love with a fellow sailor; they married and opened an inn named the Three Horseshoes.

For the first time in her life, Read lived as a woman. But her new husband soon died. Without many options for survival as a woman alone, she went back to sea, again disguised as a man. Known as "Sailor Read," she boarded a Dutch ship and sailed for the West Indies.

Anne Bonny came from wealth. She was born to a prominent lawyer in County Cork, Ireland, and the family's maid, whom he left his wife to marry. Scandalized neighbors drove Anne's father to leave Ireland, new wife and baby in tow, and settle in Charleston, South Carolina. He made a fortune, bought a large plantation, and became part of Charleston's elite. When Anne was in her teens, she helped run her father's plantation.

She was strong, with a hot temper. At thirteen she supposedly stabbed a servant girl in the stomach with a table knife. Once she nearly killed a man who attacked her.

At sixteen, Anne married a sailor and smalltime pirate, James Bonny. They planned to live on her inheritance, but that plan fell apart when her father, furious about the marriage, disowned her. According to legend, she set the plantation on fire in retaliation. The Bonnys fled to what is now Nassau, in the Bahamas, a notorious hub for pirates.

So what did Mary Read and Anne Bonny have in common? "Calico" Jack Rackham, an otherwise average pirate who dressed entirely in clothes made of coarse white cloth from India.

While in the Bahamas, Anne began hanging out with the local pirates and fell in love with Calico Jack. He offered to buy Anne from James Bonny in a "wife sale," a type of divorce then common. James not only refused but complained to the governor, who sentenced Anne to be whipped for "loose behavior" and returned to her husband.

Instead, Anne and Rackham eloped. They stole a ship anchored in the harbor, renamed it *Revenge,* and easily rallied a crew to go pirating. Anne took part in raids alongside the males and was by all accounts competent, respected, and good in combat. She donned men's clothes, which made it easier to do her job, gave her a more intimidating appearance during raids, and prevented unwanted attention if a raid went badly. Since the popular superstition at the time was that women aboard ships brought bad luck, she would have had to prove her courage over and over.

Over the next three years, she and Rackham stole several ships and accumulated treasure. They were known to go out of their way to treat their victims with respect. One of the ships they attacked held the sailor Mary Read, and so the two women met at last.

Read was given the choice to turn pirate or die, the typical way pirates were recruited. It's not clear when everyone found out she was a woman. But she and Bonny quickly became friends, touring the Caribbean as part of Rackham's crew of fourteen.

The two wore women's clothes except during raids, when each wore a man's jacket, long pants, and a handkerchief tied around her head, a pistol in one hand and a sword in the other. Mary was especially adept with her sword and once easily killed a man who challenged a boyfriend of hers to a duel.

Both women were described as physically robust. With little machinery onboard, they would have loaded and unloaded cargo, pumped out excess water, set the heavy sails, and done other tasks that were not for wimps.

Their biggest challenge may have been using the "bathroom," a crude platform set up over the water in the front of the ship.

The gang went on to attack fishing boats and merchant ships, garnering such petty hauls as fifty rolls of tobacco and nine bags of sweet red peppers. Between raids they partied—at least the men did, drinking and lounging below deck.

Merchants on land began pressuring the government to do something about the "coasts being infested by those hell-hounds the pirates." Finally, the governor of Jamaica sent forty-five men to capture the *Revenge* and its crew. During the surprise attack, Rackham and his men were reported to be so drunk that they had passed out in the ship's hull.

Only two pirates remained on deck: Read and Bonny, sober and fighting with flair. Perhaps they were so used to proving their courage that not fighting back wasn't an option. They managed to hold off the troops, but for only a short time before everyone was captured.

During a sensational trial in Jamaica, Rackham and the whole crew were sentenced to hang. Witnesses of their attacks testified that the two women "were both very profligate, cursing and swearing much, and very ready and willing to do anything." No one accused them of murder, but captives testified they were "in fear of their lives" and that the women, armed with pistol and sword, were just as aggressive as the men. Disapproval of the women would have been intense—they had broken every rule of society, including wearing men's clothes, which to some was the most shocking act of all.

Read and Bonny offered no defense and asked no questions until the sentencing phase. Then they spoke up to "plead their bellies," saying they were both pregnant. It is not known whether they were lying. Both received a stay of execution until they gave birth.

Mary Read died in prison, either from a fever or during childbirth.

While in prison Anne Bonny made one of the most famous pirate statements ever. When Rackham asked to see her one last time before his hanging, she fired back, "I am sorry to see you there, but if you had fought like a man, you need not be hanged like a dog."

She was never executed, but history doesn't tell us what happened to her. It's unlikely she took a new name and went back to piracy, which would have attracted attention. Some believe her wealthy father came to her rescue and paid a ransom for her release, and that she went on to marry a respectable citizen and have eight children.

Yet one more theory is that the governor secretly granted her a pardon on the condition that she leave the islands, along with a doctor she had fallen for, a former captive she had saved from death. Two days later, the couple reportedly left for Norfolk, Virginia, and from there joined a party of pioneers heading west. Then they simply disappeared—and in the early days of American history, this was not hard to do.

BURIED TREASURE

Four years after the trial in Jamaica, Captain Charles Johnson's *A General History of the Robberies and Murders of the Most Notorious Pyrates* was published. It prominently featured long biographies of Read and Bonny. Some of his details are confirmed by the only reliable document, the transcript of their trial, but some remain disputed. Different from the mostly religious books published at the time, Johnson's book was an instant bestseller and made Read and Bonny famous. Pirating had been so exclusively male—as was going to sea, something a boy did to "make a man" of himself—that readers were spellbound.

In 1978, Anne Bonny's life story was printed as a tiny children's book inserted into boxes of Shredded Wheat cereal. That book inspired *The Woman Pirates,* a play performed later that year by the Royal Shakespeare Company.

LEAST LIKELY TO BE A PIRATE
STEDE BONNET

1689–1718

*English gentleman whose early midlife crisis
led to raiding ships*

MOST PIRATES didn't have neighbors, but Stede Bonnet did—and his were appalled. At twenty-nine, not even into middle age, he seemed to have everything. He owned a profitable sugar plantation near Bridgetown in Barbados. He had a wife (his former neighbor), although she was rumored to be a nagging one. He'd been a respectable major in the army, with a successful career. He was a well-educated book lover. He was already rich, with no need to rob anyone. He had plenty of options in life, unlike the average pirate.

One day he decided he'd rather be capturing booty at sea.

Bridgetown's polite society found the move scandalizing. Certainly, Bonnet didn't seem to know what he was doing. Instead of stealing a ship or using other devious means to acquire one, Bonnet primly bought one. He named the ten-gun vessel *Revenge* and hired about seventy sailors on salary. Paying wages to his crew was another bizarre thing for a pirate to do. When his ship stocked up on supplies, Bonnet paid in cash instead of not paying at all. And unlike the average illiterate pirate, he filled his cabin with books.

In light of his lack of experience, it surprised many that he captured four ships near Virginia, New York, and the Carolinas in his first few weeks. But in general this unconventional pirate was only so-so at his new profession.

Then he entered into a partnership with, of all people, Blackbeard. Instead of laughing at him, the fearsome pirate seemed to like Bonnet. Perhaps he was flattered by this wannabe, or saw him as easy prey. The two prowled together for a time, as pirates sometimes did, with Bonnet staying on Blackbeard's *Queen Anne's Revenge* instead of his own *Revenge.* It was said that Bonnet spent his time reading and wandering the decks in his "morning gown," or pajamas.

It's not hard to imagine how Blackbeard tricked the distracted pirate out of his share of the bounty they captured. Blackbeard took off, and Bonnet went in pursuit, but had no luck. He turned for help to the governor of North Carolina, who was persuaded to grant him a pardon and give him a letter legally allowing him to attack Spanish ships.

Bonnet was apparently confused, because he did not limit his pirating to the despised Spanish. He renamed his ship the *Royal James,* called himself Captain Thomas, and attacked nine more ships. He was captured, almost by accident, by troops out to get Blackbeard, a much bigger fish in the pirate pond. Bonnet put up a five-hour cannon fight, which resulted in eighteen fatalities.

He was, of course, sentenced to death. Despite a long, heartfelt letter to the governor begging for mercy, the pirate whom the judge called "a man of letters" was hanged. Sympathetic women in the crowd wept as he died—and so did Bonnet, holding a nosegay bouquet as a symbol of repentance.

Bonnet's pirate career had lasted only a year. As well read as he was, he failed to keep a journal, so we have no idea why he left his comfortable life—except, perhaps, to prove that anyone can have a pirate fantasy.

A RUBY AS BIG AS A HEN'S EGG
BLACK SAM BELLAMY

1689?–1717

English pirate most famous for his ship, the Whydah

SAM BELLAMY'S childhood was tough. As one of six children brought up by their father in rural poverty, he started working when he was ten. He began his career on the water as a sailor, then turned pirate, with mates calling him Black Sam for his long black hair. Evidently popular, he was elected captain and went on to capture fifty ships in a year.

Before it was Black Sam's pirate ship, the *Whydah* started out as an English slave vessel, carrying six hundred shackled Africans from a port city on the Ivory Coast to be sold in Jamaica. By the time Black Sam caught sight of this ship, it no longer had human cargo. Instead, it carried bags of precious indigo, rare African gold jewelry, ingredients for much-needed quinine to fight malaria, hundreds of elephant tusks, bags of gold dust, a ruby rumored to be as big as a hen's egg, and a lot of money.

It took Bellamy three days of chasing around the Caribbean, but the capture of the *Whydah* made every man on his crew rich and is considered one of the largest pirate prizes ever. Bellamy converted the three-hundred-ton, eighteen-gun slaver to a pirate ship, declaring it a "free ship for free men!" Half of his 146-member crew were former slaves who had turned pirate.

The story is that Black Sam had a romantic purpose for the *Whydah*. Now that he was a man of means at age twenty-nine, he was on his way to propose to his girlfriend in Cape Cod. But he ran smack into the greatest storm then on record. In eighty-mile-an-hour winds, rocked by fifty-foot waves, the *Whydah* hit a sandbar and broke into pieces. For days afterward pirate corpses washed up on the Massachusetts shore. There were only two known survivors, and Black Sam was not one of them.

The wreckage stayed at the bottom of the ocean for 267 years. In 1984, Barry Clifford, a Cape Cod native haunted as a boy by Black Sam's tale, led a diving crew that used sonar to locate the wreck.

The thousands of artifacts they retrieved include the bell known to be the *Whydah*'s, making this the only proven pirate wreck so far. The discovery reveals a lot. Pirates liked games: backgammon, dice, various card games. They played music, with drums, trumpets, and flutes. Pirates really did find treasure—some eight thousand silver coins were found, but so far not the gigantic ruby. And they shared— some of the four hundred pieces of gold jewelry had been cut apart so they could be divided equally. We see trends in fashion (necklaces, rings with multiple jewels, square belt buckles, silver collar studs) and weapons (the fanciest of pistols, tied up with three feet of silk ribbon). It's clear that rats were an issue; the hull was lined with metal to keep them out of the food. Pirates even had manners, eating off pewter plates with spoons and forks made in France. They tried to stay healthy, with medical kits that included syringes. They went barefoot, and some had small feet—the few leather shoes onboard were in good condition and men's size five.

And we know there was a nine-year-old boy aboard the *Whydah*. In 2006 his skeleton was identified as John King's. As a passenger on a captured ship, he had pleaded with his mom to let him go with Black Sam's crew. He is the youngest pirate on record.

Conajee Angria and His Sons

THE INDIAN EMPIRE of the 1700s was a mess, with local rulers in decline and Great Britain and other invaders trying to colonize the empire. Conajee Angria, a black African Muslim navy commander, took full advantage of the confusion.

Daring and aggressive, Angria turned pirate and harassed British, Dutch, and Portuguese ships in the Indian Ocean, using small boats that easily outraced large European ships. Any adventurer with sailing expertise was welcome to join him. Always practical, he even hired Europeans when he needed their skills.

Angria was an equal-opportunity thief, also forcing Indian merchants to fork over money in exchange for not sinking their ships. He became notorious as "the terror of Bombay"—every ship that wanted safe access to Bombay (now Mumbai) had to pay him. He double-crossed everyone, signed peace treaties and broke them when it was to his advantage, and reaped enormous amounts of loot. He carved castles out of solid stone on remote cliffs and islands, easily repelling British and Portuguese enemies from these powerful vantage points.

One of Angria's more audacious moves was to seize the private yacht of the director of the English East India Company and make him pay a ransom to get it back—which was very embarrassing to England. By the time he died in 1729, Angria was king of his own turf, ranging over hundreds of miles of the Arabian Sea. He had even established his own capital city in what is now Vijaydurg, on the western coast of India, with its own currency. The Angria family fortress there had a hollow space underneath, where a boat could pull in.

He left behind five sons who didn't always get along but were only too happy to continue their father's career. By 1740 the Angrias threatened the very existence of Bombay. In the 1750s, after the brothers took over twelve major British vessels, British troops joined forces with Indian groups to launch a full-on assault on the Angrias by land and sea. They destroyed sixty-five of the Angria ships, as well as the family fortress, taking away a fortune in gold, silver, and jewels.

The final blow was the capture of the last son, Toolajee. It took six man-of-war ships and eighteen smaller ones to do it, with two days and nights of continuous bombardment. That spelled the end for the Angria dynasty, perhaps the most successful pirating family ever.

With India concentrating on pirates and neglecting its navy, the power of the British became insurmountable. Today the Angrias are seen as heroes in India, for delaying British control. Conajee Angria, especially, is considered an early freedom fighter who protected India from colonial invaders.

NOT A DAMSEL IN DISTRESS

RACHEL WALL

1760–1789

*Smalltime American pirate who
preyed on ships on land and at sea*

THE LAST WOMAN to be hanged in the state of Massachusetts was a former farm girl from Carlisle, Pennsylvania. She was born Rachel Schmidt to a devout Presbyterian family. Intensely bored, she ran away, returned, then ran away a second time at age sixteen and met up with George Wall. He was dashing, but perhaps not the best influence.

They married and lived in Boston, where Rachel worked as a maid and George fished. When they found themselves with no way to pay the rent one month, they either borrowed or stole a ship and began a pirating career around the small islands off the coast of Maine.

Their technique was unusual—and very successful. They lured passing ships by flying a distress flag from their boat. Alone on deck, Rachel yelled for help, posing as the lone survivor of some trauma. Once the would-be rescuers came aboard, Wall and his crew promptly murdered them. After seizing all valuables, they sank the captured ships, along with anyone who remained aboard.

The Walls sank at least twelve New England ships, killed at least twenty-four people, and stole a fortune in cash and goods. Back in Boston, they would claim to have found money that had washed ashore after storms—and would spend most of it on parties.

Their scam ended when George was washed overboard in a hurricane. Rachel raised the distress flag—for real this time—and was rescued. Over the next seven years, she worked as a maid again in Boston. By day, that is.

At night she snuck aboard ships docked at Boston's wharf and raided their cabins while crews were sleeping. This would have taken serious courage. Once, she crept into the room of a snoring captain and calmly reached underneath his mattress, coming up with a pile of gold. Another time she made off with a silver watch that hung directly above a sleeping captain's head, as well as the silver buckles off his shoes, and a pile of coins. The bathrooms in the captains' quarters, she discovered, were the spots to find the best stuff.

No one ever caught Rachel on a ship, but one day someone accused her of robbing a woman on a Boston street. At twenty-nine she was arrested and tried for highway robbery. On the stand she confessed to piracy, swearing she had never killed anyone—but she denied highway robbery.

The night before her death by hanging, she issued a statement of warning to other young women: Stay away from bad company.

Necklaces of Severed Heads
Madame Cheng

1775–1844

Chinese commander of two thousand ships
and the largest pirate gang in history

IMAGINE THE SIGHT looming on the horizon: hundreds of ships, each with twenty cannons, and thousands of screaming pirates—men, women, and children. All under the command of one remarkable woman.

Over and over, Madame Cheng proved she would do whatever it took to survive—an incredible feat in China at the time, where women were treated harshly.

She was a Cantonese prostitute, reported to be beautiful. We don't know her name before she married Cheng I and became "wife of Cheng" at about age twenty-six. Some historians say he was hunchbacked and unattractive. But he commanded a pirate fleet, and marrying him was one way for his wife to escape restrictions on land. He came from a pirate family, and fled Vietnamese civil war to gain control of some two hundred boats attacking vessels in the South China Sea.

Madame Cheng joined her husband onboard. Many Chinese sailors took their wives with them to help with steering and other tasks; some families lived their whole lives in cramped conditions on boats. The Chengs set about uniting rival gangs into a confederation organized by flags of six colors: red, black, white, blue, yellow, and green. Each fleet had to agree to a code of conduct and stick to its own area.

Based in Canton, the dynamic couple controlled the red flag fleet personally. From Hong Kong to the Vietnam border, they attacked lucrative salt ships and other merchant ships, taking cannons and gunpowder wherever they went. They had two sons and adopted another, Chang Pao.

By the time Cheng I was washed overboard in a gale, their confederation numbered four hundred ships and thousands of pirates. After some expert manipulation, Madame Cheng was elected the new head. One writer described her outfit at her election: robes with gold-embroidered dragons writhing over backgrounds of rich purple and red, sewn with bits of ivory and jade, her husband's war helmet on her head, his swords in her sash.

She made the big decisions, putting Chang Pao in command of day-to-day operations. She also married and had a son with him, which solidified the family's control of the fleet. He became a popular captain and a flashy dresser, with purple silk robes and a black turban.

Instituting an elaborate, formal structure, Madame Cheng organized the largest pirate gang in history, eventually commanding two thousand ships. Newspapers of the time reported her exploits. Unlike her husband, she wasn't afraid to attack powerful European ships. She established coastal "offices" to collect fees she imposed. She killed thousands and captured others, especially rich merchants she could hold for ransom. Alongside rivers, she looted whole villages, and those that resisted were burned to the ground. During attacks, her pirates would behead villagers—after stringing a cord through the pigtails, they wore the heads as necklaces.

Madame Cheng's ships were flat-bottomed, square-sailed boats known as junks, with as many as twenty oars for rowing up rivers. Each pirate was allowed a berth only about four feet square, even if he had a wife and children in there with him. Curling up at night was a necessity. When they weren't raiding, pirates spent their days gambling, playing cards, smoking opium. Unless better provisions had been stolen, a typical meal would be red rice, sometimes with salted fish. If they were hungry enough, they would add boiled caterpillars or rats to the rice. Some pirates believed that eating the hearts of their enemies with rice would increase their courage; some also believed that a sprinkle of garlic water would protect them from being shot. Madame Cheng believed that serving her crews wine mixed with gunpowder before raids increased their ferocity.

She was a stricter disciplinarian than any other known pirate captain. She was to get four-fifths of all booty. Crew members who went ashore without permission would get their ears slit—doing it a second time meant death. She was big on flogging. She must have been simply terrifying. One of her most important captains, ashamed at having survived a failed raid, committed suicide at her feet.

As the Manchu dynasty was losing control of the country, it was increasingly easy for Madame Cheng to repel every attempt to defeat her. In one year the Chinese navy lost sixty-three ships to her attacks, and the government resorted to using private fishing vessels for its work. The British Royal Navy was supposedly patrolling

the waters, but that was also a weak presence. Once, she successfully blockaded Macao, the city held by Portugal. During the several weeks it took the Portuguese navy to drive her away, the city got down to a two-day supply of rice.

She enjoyed three years of success, amassing a fortune. Finally, Chinese officials grew so desperate that they offered unconditional amnesty to any pirate who surrendered. Madame Cheng decided this would be a great moment to quit. Her colored fleets had begun fighting one another, weakening her force.

Taking a group of pirate women and children with her, she arrived unarmed for a meeting with the governor general. In two days of negotiations, she obtained pardons for 17,000 of her men (just 126 were executed, and several hundred banished), got Chang Pao a lieutenancy in the Chinese army, and retired with her fortune intact.

Madame Cheng carried on as a somewhat more respectable member of society for another twenty years, running a gambling house until she died at the relatively old age of seventy.

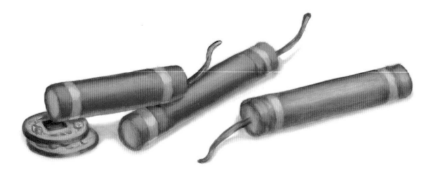

BURIED TREASURE

Madame Cheng may have inspired two Chinese women pirates of the twentieth century. La Hon-Cho, who may have been of noble birth, commanded sixty ships in 1921, when she was in her midtwenties.

Later in the 1920s, Lai Choi San ("Mountain of Wealth") led a famous pirate gang on twelve ships while in her thirties, with two sons in tow. She set off fireworks before each raid, and it was said that she never smiled. She in turn inspired the character Dragon Lady in *Terry and the Pirates,* a 1940s comic strip.

WITTY IN THREE LANGUAGES

JEAN LAFFITE

1782?–1823?

Clever, colorful Frenchman who ruled the New Orleans underworld

A CRIMINAL such as Jean Laffite couldn't have asked for a better place to operate than 1800s New Orleans. Louisiana didn't become one of the United States until 1812, and its legendary city was a bubbling brew of slaves, free blacks, Creoles, Spaniards, and Frenchmen, with no one much in control. The few American officials around were distracted by war with Britain, corrupt, or new in town.

By 1809 Jean was listed as the owner of a blacksmith shop in the city, along with his older half brother and trusty partner, Pierre. They were definitely not smithies, but were using the shop as a cover for their real business: smuggling goods and slaves.

The Laffite brothers had made their way from the vineyards of Bordeaux, France, seeking opportunity after the French Revolution. They had been taught the basics of reading and writing; perhaps more important, they had learned to depend on themselves. In the every-man-for-himself atmosphere of New Orleans, they flourished.

Jean had acquired sea captain experience while Pierre stuck to managing operations on land. After Pierre suffered a stroke at age forty, leaving him partially paralyzed, Jean was in firm control of the business. They set up their own pirate kingdom in the barely inhabited swamps and islands of Barataria Bay, fifty miles south of New Orleans. Anyone looking for deals on stolen goods was instructed to seek out "the notorious Captain Laffite." With between three and ten ships and between three hundred and five hundred men, Jean preyed on any ship they could take—British, American, Spanish—with no discrimination. The Laffites were slick businessmen playing all sides.

The illegal sale of Africans was most profitable, but also of value were hauls of logwood, indigo, cochineal, fine fabrics, coffee, sugar, and household goods. Under cover of night, the brothers sold goods through a network of accomplices who traded with upstanding citizens in New Orleans. Then Jean went back to his island, where he had the only house—his crew lived in about forty temporary shacks.

The Laffites perfected the art of eluding capture. They wore disguises, hid in wells, swam to shore when necessary. Whenever they were summoned to court, they never showed up. Once they were both arrested—and then simply released, perhaps because they were so skilled at lavish flattery. Another day, as Pierre languished in jail, Jean wrote shrewd letters to newspapers claiming his brother's innocence while secretly coordinating colleagues to break Pierre out.

Jean was always flouting authority, even joking around. When one governor offered a five-hundred-dollar reward for his capture, Jean doubled that amount and offered it for the capture of the governor. He put up posters announcing the reward around town, noting at the bottom that he was "only *jesting.*"

When he came in to New Orleans from his island, Jean stayed with Pierre and his biracial girlfriend and their children, or else at a boardinghouse. Other boarders found him good company at meals, witty in three languages. One friend said, "His manners were highly polished, and in his pleasant moods, one who did not know him would have suspected him for being anything but a pirate." He dressed stylishly, had an otter-skin hat, and was a favorite at parties. He was more than six feet tall, with unusually white teeth and pale skin (for a pirate), very small hands and feet, and a habit of shutting one eye while he spun stories for hours. (He may have been blind in that eye.) He lived for the moment, was usually in debt, and had one son with his longtime girlfriend, a biracial woman named Catherine.

Violence was not Jean's style. He treated captured crews with respect, even fetching a doctor if anyone was wounded, and never killed anyone. He ruled his pirates with strict discipline but fairness, and had few problems with them. "I understand the management of such men perfectly," he once said.

Jean was part gangster, part hero. The hero part came when British officials offered him money and a pardon in return for his help in attacking New Orleans. Instead of taking them up on the lucrative offer, he warned Americans about the attack. Yet he wasn't being a patriotic American; he was just concerned about the survival of his business. Jean had vague affection for France but was otherwise strictly apolitical.

American officials didn't pay much attention to his warning then, but later General Andrew Jackson accepted Jean's offer of aid in combat with the British. It was perhaps Jean's slickest maneuver ever. In return for manning guns on warships during the Battle of New Orleans in 1815, he and his pirates were pardoned by President James Madison.

Jean promptly resumed pirating. Amid fears of the "hellish banditti," rumors spread that he had two thousand men and a dozen ships and had to be stopped. The

official most determined to squelch Jean had been held captive in the Barbary States and had a huge grudge against pirates. In one raid Jean lost more than ten thousand gallons of wine, medicinal herbs, silk stockings, and plates and glasses. He was forced to shift his business farther away from New Orleans to Cat Island off the coast of Mississippi.

He finally settled on the lawless island of Galveston in Texas, establishing a community for and funded by pirates. Now they could raid in the still-disputed territories around Mexico, Texas, and Cuba, avoiding American officials. As usual, they double-crossed and triple-crossed everyone—Spain, Mexican rebels in Texas, and the United States—taking money from all sides. Jean always claimed never to have plundered an American vessel, but this wasn't true.

Galveston had a pirates-only pool hall, a coffeehouse, shops, a fortress that commanded the harbor with cannon in place, and several wooden houses—Jean's was the nicest. He ate well every night, the table set with china plates and linen, and drank fine wines. He had grand plans for his new community, but as the American government cracked down on piracy, he was forced to evacuate. He agreed to leave the island without a fight, reportedly taking immense amounts of treasure with him and burning everything as he left. Rumors grew that he stashed gold and jewelry in the marshes, swamps, and bayous of Galveston Bay.

After that, Jean Laffite was never heard from again. It is believed he went to Central America to continue his raids. At age forty-one, Jean was killed, apparently by gunfire, during a Spanish attack on his ship. (Pierre had died of a fever two years earlier.) Ironically, Jean's last ship was one with a perfectly legal commission from the navy of Colombia. For years afterward, rumors circulated that he was still alive—doing something dashing and probably illegal.

BURIED TREASURE

References to Jean Laffite appear frequently in movies and elsewhere in popular culture. The breakfast cereal character Cap'n Crunch has a pirate enemy named Jean LaFoote. At Disneyland in California, "Laffite's Landing" is where the Pirates of the Caribbean ride (inspiration for the famous movies) begins.

In the 1950s, a manuscript known as the "Journal of Jean Laffite" surfaced in the hands of a man claiming to be his descendant. This diary claims that Jean was Jewish through descent from a grandmother—and that he faked his death, later living in several American states, raising a family, and dying in St. Louis, Missouri, in the 1840s. The authenticity of the journal is hotly debated among Laffite scholars. He may be the only pirate to have inspired a scholarly society dedicated to uncovering more information about him: the Laffite Society of Galveston.

THE *BLACK JOKE*
BENITO DE SOTO

1800?–1832

*Bloodthirsty Portuguese outlaw often called
one of the last pirates*

BENITO DE SOTO proved himself as a leader by organizing a mutiny. Off southwest Africa, he and the rest of the crew took over their Argentinean slave ship. He was as violent as his mates, or perhaps more so: During that night's victory party, the others elected him captain—after he shot the mate who had helped him.

He renamed his ship the *Black Joke* and proceeded to cross the Atlantic to sell his cargo of slaves. Then he sailed south, attacking Spanish ships on the coast of South America. After that he headed back across the Atlantic to snatch boats laden with tea, opium, and spices from India and the Far East. His attitude was no-nonsense—authorities could trace his path by noticing the line of missing ships. For the last five years of his life, Benito de Soto was the most wanted pirate in the Atlantic.

He was fond of locking everyone below deck before he sank a ship, guaranteeing that all would die. Once when a captured sailor helped him pilot the *Black Joke* safely into a harbor, de Soto thanked him, then turned around and shot him in the head. Even his African cabin boy was a target, with de Soto in the habit of hitting him with his telescope.

In a particularly brutal attack, de Soto spotted the *Morning Star* as it was sailing from Ceylon to England with a cargo of coffee and cinnamon. He took over the ship, killed most of the passengers, and locked the rest in the hold. De Soto then wrecked the ship, planning as usual to sink it and leave no evidence or witnesses. But the prisoners managed to escape and somehow prevented the *Morning Star* from sinking.

The joke was on de Soto when the *Black Joke* was wrecked off the coast of Spain. He and his men went to the island of Gibraltar to recover, staying at a rundown inn. Some of his *Morning Star* victims were staying there too, and de Soto was promptly arrested. At his trial in Cadiz, the star testimony against him came from his cabin boy.

At de Soto's hanging, he showed nerves of steel by arranging the noose around his own neck. After his death his head was stuck on a pike as the traditional warning to other sailors contemplating a life of piracy. Perhaps the warning succeeded, as de Soto is considered one of the last pirates we know by name.

LONG JOHN SILVER

*Appeared as a character in a book
first published in 1883*

SOME OF WHAT we believe about pirates comes from the imagination of a sickly, gentle writer.

Robert Louis Stevenson wanted his stepson to like him. One rainy August day in the Scottish mountains, twelve-year-old Lloyd was painting with his box of watercolors. Stevenson amused him by drawing a map of an imaginary Caribbean island. As they both added to the map, Stevenson started making up a wild tale—about the deserted island, buried treasure, a sea cook with only one leg, lots of violence, a song ending "Yo ho ho and a bottle o' rum." Lloyd was captivated.

Stevenson wrote it all down, telling the story in the voice of a young boy, Jim Hawkins. Three days later he had three chapters done. Lloyd continued to add his ideas, requesting that no women appear in the story. Fifteen chapters into it, Stevenson ran out of story. In October he traveled to Switzerland and began writing again at white heat, a chapter a day.

The tale was first published in a magazine, but readers didn't care much for it. The story wasn't popular until it was revised and published in 1883 as a novel called *Treasure Island*.

The book mentions some real pirates—William Kidd, Blackbeard, Black Bart—but is most famous for conjuring up the colorful Long John Silver. Both hero and villain, Silver is a cook with a parrot always perched on his shoulder. He's lost one of his legs and uses a crutch to get around. He's a criminal but not as evil as some of the actual pirates of history.

Like today's Captain Jack Sparrow from the Pirates of the Caribbean movies, Silver is not real. Stevenson's goal was to invent a character that was both funny and cutthroat. He didn't know any real pirates, so he based Long John Silver on a fellow writer. Lloyd later described that writer as "a great, glowing, massive-shouldered fellow with a big red beard and a crutch . . . astoundingly clever, and with a laugh that rolled like music."

Stevenson borrowed other elements from earlier writers, such as Edgar Allan Poe, Washington Irving, and Daniel Defoe. In turn, he influenced his good friend J. M. Barrie in creating *Peter Pan* and its notorious pirate, Captain Hook.

Because of *Treasure Island*—and the numerous fanciful Hollywood movies based on it—we have the illusion that pirates were basically likable outlaws, always striding around accompanied by cute parrots (seamen did enjoy bringing back parrots as souvenirs from the tropics), burying treasure on deserted islands (seldom, if ever, did a real pirate do this, much less draw a map to it), and making captives walk the plank (there are few records of this ever happening).

Stevenson did get a lot right with his vivid descriptions of sailing and life at sea. As a child he had accompanied his father and grandfather, both lighthouse keepers, on inspections around Scotland. All his life, between bouts of serious illness (when he wrote his books in bed), he had numerous seafaring adventures of his own—legal ones.

Treasure Island turned out to be Stevenson's first successful novel. Eleven years after its publication, he died at age forty-four, having created the ultimate pirate.

FOR FURTHER READING

Bawlf, R. Samuel. *The Secret Voyage of Sir Francis Drake, 1577–1580*. New York: Penguin, 2003.

Breverton, Terry. *Admiral Sir Henry Morgan: King of the Buccaneers*. Gretna, La.: Pelican, 2005.

———. *Black Bart Roberts: The Greatest Pirate of Them All*. Gretna, La.: Pelican, 2004.

Burnett, John S. *Dangerous Waters: Modern Piracy and Terror on the High Seas*. New York: Dutton, 2002.

Chambers, Anne. *Granuaile: The Life and Times of Grace O'Malley c. 1530–1603*. Dublin, Ireland: Wolfhound Press, 1998.

Clifford, Barry, with Paul Perry. *Expedition* Whydah: *The Story of the World's First Excavation of a Pirate Treasure Ship and the Man Who Found Her*. New York: HarperCollins, 1999.

Cordingly, David. *Under the Black Flag: The Romance and the Reality of Life Among the Pirates*. New York: Random House, 1995.

Davis, William C. *The Pirates Laffite: The Treacherous World of the Corsairs of the Gulf*. San Diego: Harcourt, 2005.

Konstam, Angus. *Blackbeard: America's Most Notorious Pirate*. New York: Wiley, 2006.

———. *The History of Pirates*. Guilford, Conn.: Lyons Press, 2002.

Lorimer, Sara. *Booty: Girl Pirates on the High Seas*. San Francisco: Chronicle Books, 2002.

Preston, Diana and Michael Preston. *A Pirate of Exquisite Mind: Explorer, Naturalist, and Buccaneer: The Life of William Dampier*. New York: Walker, 2004.

Ritchie, Robert C. *Captain Kidd and the War Against the Pirates*. Cambridge: Harvard University Press, 1986.

Rogozinski, Jan. *Pirates: An A–Z Encyclopedia*. New York: Da Capo Press, 1996.

Stanley, Jo, ed. *Bold in Her Breeches: Women Pirates Across the Ages*. San Francisco: Pandora, 1995.

Zacks, Richard. *The Pirate Hunter: The True Story of Captain Kidd*. New York: Hyperion, 2002.

9